Silent Observer

Written and Illustrated by Christy MacKinnon

Kendall Green Publications   Gallaudet University Press

Kendall Green Publications
An imprint of Gallaudet University Press
Washington, DC 20002

Published 1993. Second printing, 1994
Printed in Hong Kong
Designed by Kathy Klingaman Cunningham
Calligraphy by Cheryl Jacobsen

Library of Congress Cataloging-in-Publication Data

MacKinnon, Christy. 1889-1981.
   Silent observer / written and illustrated by
   Christy MacKinnon.
        p.   cm.
   ISBN 1-56368-022-X (alk. paper) : $15.95
   1. MacKinnon, Christy, 1889-1981. 2.
Children, Deaf—Nova Scotia—Cape Breton
Island—Biography. I. Title.
HV2577.M33A3 1993
362.4'2'092—dc20
[B]   93-4510
                         CIP

In Memoriam

The publication of *Silent Observer* was a labor of love for Inez MacKinnon Simeone, the niece of Christy MacKinnon. It was Inez's vision and careful hand that brought this book to life as a fitting legacy for her aunt.

Inez completed the manuscript and layout for *Silent Observer* in September 1992, two months before her death. This book is dedicated to Inez Simeone and to her vision, spirit, and loyalty.

Acknowledgments

The family of Inez MacKinnon Simeone gratefully acknowledges the contributions and support of Dr. George Hagerty, Ms. Annie Holden, and the people of Stonehill College in the development of this book.

A Note to the Reader

In the spring of 1990, while I was rummaging in my basement, a weathered note fell from a parcel containing some of the artwork left to me by my aunt, Christy MacKinnon. Written in her distinctive hand, it stated simply, "When my story is told, it will be called *Silent Observer*." This simple, yet direct, message led me to examine the many packages of artwork and diary notes that had been sitting unopened for several years. My discovery of the treasure within these packages provided me the opportunity to make Aunt Christy's directive a reality, and what better title to use than her own.

Christy MacKinnon was an extraordinary woman. As you will learn, she was a talented artist and a wonderful storyteller. Her life's accomplishments were made all the more remarkable because she was deaf.

Silent Observer is a book to be shared with friends and family, people young and old. Although most of the story takes place in an era long past, the themes of courage, humor, and wonder at the world are timeless.

As an artist and a writer, Christy MacKinnon never denied the child within. It is a special quality that permeates each page of this touching memoir. I hope you will find as much joy in reading about Christy's life as I have.

Inez MacKinnon Simeone
Milton, Massachusetts

Christy MacKinnon

Christy MacKinnon was born in the farming community of Boisdale, Cape Breton Island, Nova Scotia, on October 28, 1889. Raised in a very large family, Christy lost her hearing from a serious illness at the age of two.

Her early education took place under the guidance of her father, the local schoolmaster, in a one-room schoolhouse that served all the children of the Boisdale countryside. In 1900, Christy's father enrolled her in the Halifax School for the Deaf. Christy's family and teachers in Halifax recognized her artistic talent, so while she attended school she also studied at the Victoria School for the Arts.

After graduating from the Halifax School for the Deaf in 1908, the talented young artist continued to study at the Victoria School and undertook work commissioned by local citizens.

In 1912, Christy traveled to the United States, accepting a scholarship to study at the Boston Museum of Fine Arts. Several years later, she moved to New York City, where she stayed from 1915 to 1919. Christy continued studying art and worked as a freelance illustrator.

Christy MacKinnon returned to the Halifax School for the Deaf in 1920 to teach art, and she remained at the school until her marriage in 1928 to John Maxcy, a New York printer who was also deaf.

Christy and John lived in New York, where Christy established herself as a leading illustrator, working for the firm of F.A.O. Schwarz. In 1948, Christy and John Maxcy retired to Sutton Mills, New Hampshire. There the artist continued to paint and draw.

After the death of her husband in 1952, Christy moved to Natick, Massachusetts, to live with her sister Sadie (MacKinnon) Theriault, who also had been deafened by a childhood disease. It was at the Natick residence that Christy applied her special artistic gifts, recording memories of childhood in the form that has become this book.

Christy MacKinnon died in 1981, leaving a rich legacy as an artist, a storyteller, and above all, a generous friend.

I was born, like my seven brothers and sisters, in a house atop a hill overlooking lovely Bras d'Or Lakes in Cape Breton Island, Nova Scotia, Canada. The year was 1889.

Our farm was near the village of Boisdale. My father was the only teacher of Boisdale's one-room schoolhouse.

That winter was put down in history as one of the severest ever. My mother wrote in a letter that my sisters Mary, Sadie, and I were just recovering from a siege of whooping cough. In those days, we did not have medicines for many diseases. Sadie lost some hearing; I lost all of mine.

Ma didn't believe I was deaf. One day, I was outside playing in the sand when a family horse was freed from his traces to run to pasture. I was in the way. I couldn't hear my mother's frightened call as the frisky horse leaped over me. Only the shadow cast above made me look up in surprise. My mother cried and cried in her apron.

Ma died giving birth to her eighth child, our brother Steven. I watched bewildered as sleeping Ma was taken away in a black box in the sunshine with the blue sea below. The wind blew, billowing women's skirts and flapping men's pants and short coats. Those wearing derbies held on to them with both hands. Ma was only 36; I was 3. Goodbye, Ma!

Aunt Sarah came to take care of us. She certainly had her hands full. One afternoon, as she was washing clothes, she heard my sister Meg crying. Meg timidly told her that I was in the well. Aunt Sarah rushed to the well and hauled me out.

After that, she took me every-where she went.

After Ma died, we moved in with Grandma and Grandpa, who had a farm near ours. Baby Steven went to live with Aunt Sarah.

That first winter the house was full of people; it was the time of railroad building. I woke every morning to the hustle of boots on the floor and the smells of cooking. At spinning bees and tucking parties, Grandma was forever talking and working in a hurry, from dawn to dark.

Soon after moving, I went out to explore. I wandered into the barnyard and found myself gazing at the circling legs, the tails, and the gimlet eyes of fifteen cows. Grandma shouted a warning to Pa, who rushed out of the barn. He paled when he saw my red dress beneath a cow. Striding slowly, he grabbed me and held me high above the cows' backs and horns. Then, he airlifted me to Grandma.

Grandma let out angry words, but you cannot control a small deaf child with voice commands. Besides, I couldn't understand her because she spoke Gaelic. Pa was angry with my sister Mary for not watching me. I knew right away that I had done something wrong. Mary showed me exactly what later on. I stayed out of the barnyard for a long time after that.

I spent a lot of time with my sister Sadie, who was two years older. We made up our own home sign language to share what we saw.

During the winter months, we were kept indoors, sometimes for days at a stretch. We were always near the kitchen window, which faced the road and the barn, the railroad and the lake yonder. Here, we gained an excellent education watching the people passing by and the goings-on in the barnyard. Sadie and I knew our neighbors by the way they looked and acted, their horses, and their vehicles. Everyone in the family would laugh with recognition when I used gestures to describe the "red beard man," "the lame horse man," and many others.

It was Pa, though, who loomed largest in my world. He was a gifted farmer and teacher. Although young to be a school-master, he taught many adults to read and write, too.

To all of us children, Pa was bigger than life.

Pa's example commanded our respect and molded us. We did chores together, bringing in firewood, rolling cloth strips into balls for hooking, and helping each other with school-work. Every afternoon at 5:00 I would bring the cows in from the pasture. The cows were always ready to come home. They told time better than our old kitchen clock!

Sadie and I loved to explore. The barn and the yard around it held special mystery and delight for us.

One beautiful summer day, a Sunday, we discovered a new bull in the barn. We had put on our new dresses, and we just had to parade before the cows—that's when we saw the bull. We stared at him and he stared back at us. Then, the bull let out a roar that shook the barn and frightened us near to death! We ran out of the barn and bumped right into Pa. He laughed and laughed. He pointed to our dresses and made the sign for *red*. "Bulls don't like red," he told us. It was a lesson we never forgot.

Most of the time, Sadie and I stayed with Grandma. She made all our clothes, even our socks, and we saw the whole process of wool goods made from the back of the sheep to the loom upstairs. First, Grandma sheared the sheep, then she washed the wool and carded it. At her spinning wheel in the kitchen, she would sit and spin, talk and sing. Sadie and I would sit on the floor in a stream of warm winter sunlight and roll the spun wool into balls. Finally, Grandma would make the cloth on her loom.

Grandma and I understood each other through smiles and gestures, and even though we could not talk, she tried to teach me responsibility. One day, she gave me a little pail half-filled with oatmeal water. With a sweet smile, she led me to the open door and pointed to the bent old man working in the field—my grandfather. I obeyed her happily, walking slowly so as not to spill the contents of the pail.

Grandpa did not hear me approaching, and I could not call out to him. He kept on swinging his scythe, cutting down the straw. Each time he took a step forward, I followed behind him, stepping into his huge footprints. Finally he paused for a rest. I quickly moved in front of him and held out the pail. His startled expression changed into a broad smile. He patted my head lightly

and took a long drink from the pail. Then, he gave me another pat and pointed me toward the house. I walked back to find Grandma still in the doorway waiting for my return.

When the weather was good, Sadie and I stayed outside near the brook, the mill, or the road bridge. All the other children went to school except Johnny, who was even younger than I. Grandma didn't mind that we were outside, but she worried because we couldn't hear her call us. Somehow, though, it seemed that even the farm animals looked out for us.

One day, I found out that a new lamb had been born in the barn. I rushed out the front door to go see it. But inside the pen, the big boss ram ran up to me and stopped me. He bowed down and nudged me. The ram gently pushed me again, all the way back to the gate. It was almost as if he were saying, "Go home, little one."

After several incidents like that, Grandma and Pa decided that the best way to keep Sadie and me out of mischief was to send us to school. I was four and Sadie was six. Our sister Bee was put in charge of us, but we were also under Pa's watchful eye all day long.

It was a mile from home to school. The walk was made all the more fun because our oldest brother, Alec, lead a MacKinnon chorus all the way to the schoolyard. Pa, who always arrived early, could hear us from afar. He would meet us at the door shaking his head and smiling, and he'd jokingly comment on how we sang off key. Sadie and I would sign to Pa that we couldn't hear, so he could not blame us for what he heard. Pa would laugh and laugh.

All of Boisdale's children through the age of fourteen were educated in a one-room schoolhouse. Pa was a very organized teacher, alternating the lessons of his younger charges with the work of his older students.

Sadie and I had our own slates and pencils and penmanship books. We practiced writing all day long. We loved school, especially Fridays because Pa always seemed more relaxed on Fridays. He would tell stories and sing songs with the boys and girls.

When I was four, Pa decided to move our house! First, the house was rolled down the hill next to Grandma and Grandpa's house. It sat there on stilts for about a year. Then, one morning, we awoke because the house was swaying. Sadie and I dressed quickly to see what was happening. From our open front door we stared at the men and horses as they pulled the house down the road. Suddenly, Pa appeared, chest high, at the door. He lifted us down to the ground and sent us to Grandma and Grandpa's house for breakfast.

We all were astounded. We stared with wonder at the house rolling by. The horses tugged, their muscles bulging, as men placed logs under the house.

Men and horses worked in harmony.

Pa picked a beautiful location for our home. He planted apple trees and a row of cranberry bushes along the driveway. Soon after we moved, workmen came to build two wings on the house, adding seven rooms. Some evenings after we ate, Pa washed up, put on his Sunday suit, and drove off. Alec and Bee whispered to each other, but they never explained where Pa went. Later, I learned he was visiting a widow who lived five miles away.

One of our happiest days after our mother died was when Pa brought home his new wife. We were so excited, we ran out to pick flowers and berries for her. Alec went fishing and brought her a string of trout. Our eagerness to please our new mother charmed her. We all called her Mama, and it didn't take us long to love her.

Mama learned to use gestures and facial expressions with me, and she talked clearly so I could read her lips. I loved her even more for this and did whatever I could to please her.

Mama appreciated all our gifts—no matter what kind. Her eyes sparkled and she clapped her hands when we brought her eggs, flowers, berries, and even wood chips. She used the wood chips for kindling in the oven before she baked biscuits. Her biscuits were always high and fluffy.

Mama baked us our first cake. Johnny, Sadie, Meg, and I stood around the table watching as she prepared the batter. At first she was so touched by our fascination that tears welled up in her eyes. Then, she began to laugh. She let each of us lick the bowl.

One day soon after the wedding, Mama and Pa drove away in the carriage. When they came back, they had a little girl with them. Pa explained that she was Mama's daughter Cassie and she was four years old. We were delighted to have a new sister.

About a year later, Sadie and I were awakened one night by the heat and light coming through the floor around the chimney pipe. Of course we were curious, so we went downstairs. We saw Grandma sitting in a rocker beside a cradle on the floor. She smiled at us and lifted the cradle blanket, revealing two tiny red faces. We gawked. Then, Grandma told us to go back to bed.

The next morning we ran downstairs to see the twins. We gestured to our sister Mary, asking "Where come from?" Mary signed back to us, "The doctor's bag." Though we accepted this answer, we somehow sensed that the babies belonged to Mama. Only later did someone explain that they were our new twin sister and brother.

Our Pa was well-known and respected in our town. Besides being the only teacher, he was an expert at farming. People often came to ask for his advice.

One of our neighbors, Alexander Graham Bell, was also interested in farming. Dr. Bell spent each summer across the bay from our farm. He called his farm Beinn Bhreagh. He frequently came to discuss the latest farming methods with Pa.

Dr. Bell was also interested in improving the lives of people who are deaf, and he took a special interest in Sadie and me. He was the first person to test our hearing. One day when he came to visit, he brought a rubber tube with him. He spoke to Sadie through the tube and laughed heartily when she answered back. He tried the same thing with me, but I could not hear him.

On each visit, Dr. Bell encouraged Pa to pursue the dream he held for Sadie and me—the dream of an education and a life of independence.

As the years went by, I had more and more trouble understanding what people said. I found that my abilities to understand and be understood were only as successful as others allowed.

Aside from Sadie, my brother Alec was the best storyteller in the family. Although he never really learned sign language, he made every effort to let Sadie and me know the events of the day, small or large. I recall clearly the astonishing story of a terrible electric storm and Alec acting out how it killed five milk cows under a tree.

I had a much harder time trying to understand adults, even my parents. Once, Mama sent me to the store to buy some thread. When I asked the store owner for thread, he just looked at me and asked, "What number?" When I didn't answer, he yelled again, "What number?!"

I finally understood, but I had no idea, so I bolted home (about 1 ¼ miles) to ask Mama. She said she had told me the first time, but I had not understood. This time, she showed me the number. I went back and bought the thread. After that, Mama always gave me a list when I went to the store.

Despite my deafness, I was never left out of family activities. One winter afternoon, Pa decided to exercise his big horse Dan. It was a mild, cloudy day, and the world was wrapped in pure white. The roads were not yet broken in, but Bras d'Or Lake was frozen solid. Pa came into the kitchen wearing his black, curly fur coat and told us to get ready for a sleigh ride.

After all of us were settled snugly in the straw-bedded sleigh, Pa drove out to the lake. The sun sparkled off the ice-bound sea as the horse began to run. Sleigh bells bounced on his back and sides, and white smoke poured out of his nostrils. The rush of wind tingled our faces, making them look like polished apples.

All of a sudden, the horse began to gallop, giving us a violent jolt. Poor Sadie smacked into the dashboard and got a bloody nose. Pa stood up, scissored the reins, and began roaring commands at the horse, who instantly returned to a trot. Pa turned the sleigh around and headed for home. We never went for another ice ride.

The summer I was nine, I found out how different I was from everyone else. One afternoon I was told to bring the cows home. I looked all over, but couldn't find them. So, I ran home to ask Sadie to help me. We went to the top of the hill, and she began hollering for Meena, the lead cow. Sure enough, the cows appeared and walked serenely back to the

barn. Then and there I realized that I was different. Sadie could hear, but I couldn't. The dog, the chicks, the cows, the pigs all could hear, but I couldn't. I didn't understand why, and it began to torment me. I cried and cried, unhappy most of the time.

Mama and Pa held a family council. When it was over, Bee explained that, because I was deaf, Mama and Pa would send me to a special school to learn to read books. I was to go to this school by train.

Later that year, I caught typhoid fever. I lived in isolation for three months, but I was lucky to be alive. My sister Meg was not; she caught the fever and died.

When my day of liberation from isolation arrived, Mary, Bee, and Alec came in laughing and talking. Alec showed me his shiny new boots and danced a few steps around the room. Then, he pried open the sealed door to let in the marvelous spring-scented air. I breathed it in large gulps. Mary dressed me in my red woolen dress, and it hung loosely from my shoulders. Pa and Mama escorted me to the kitchen, where they wrapped me up and sat me in the rocking chair.

I was so happy to see everyone; it felt like Thanksgiving in the house. Sadie stared at me

as if I were a ghost. Pa reassured her that I was all right now, I had just lost some weight and some of my hair!

Because of my illness, I did not go to the Halifax School for the Deaf until the fall of 1900. Finally, the day came for me to leave. Mama packed my new trunk full of newly sewn clothes, and we said a tearful good-bye. Pa and Sadie drove me to the train depot. Sadie cried and asked Pa over and over why she couldn't go with me. When the smoking monster train arrived, Pa lifted me up on the steps and the conductor hauled me in. I turned to see Sadie staring and Pa waving. Then I was surrounded by a group of girls that included my cousin Marie, who was going to the school to work.

The train trip was very long, and the steady bump of the wheels put me to sleep. When I awoke, it was dark. The coach was full of teenagers talking in sign language. Finally, after twelve hours, we arrived in Halifax. The train station was a skeleton of iron covered with glass and lit by thousands of gas lamps. Crowds of people walked everywhere, laughing with happy faces. It was new, amazing, and bewildering to me.

I felt the terrible agony of homesickness for many weeks. Several times I tried to run away. I would slip through the high grill gate and search for

the train station. But each time, someone from the school found me and took me back. One day my cousin Marie came to talk to me. She made me understand that my home was very far away and that I had to stay at the school.

My pangs of homesickness began to pass when I received a letter from home. Marie signed the letter to me and, suddenly, I was a happy child again. I made her answer the letter for me on the spot. That night, I stopped crying into my pillow.

Once over my homesickness, I began to make friends with the girls in my dormitory. Though we were forbidden to use sign language in the classroom, we always signed to each other out of school. The boys and girls I met in school became a second family to me.

I was fortunate to have a wonderful teacher, Mr. Fearon. He was the principal, and he took a special interest in me. I had arrived at school able to write the alphabet and numbers and about one hundred words. Mr. Fearon recognized my abilities and promoted me into a higher class, even though I could not read. But with teachers who knew how to teach deaf children, I learned very quickly.

Every day after school I went to Mr. Fearon's office for special tutoring in speech and lipreading. He taught me how to say each letter of the alphabet and the names for objects, like "ball." After many months of hard work, I amazed the other teachers by saying, "You put a blue book on the table."

My favorite place at the school was the big gate overlooking Gottingen Street. Even though I no longer wanted to run away, I loved to watch all the horse buggies and the people on the street. I especially liked the soldiers on parade, some in red uniforms, some in khaki. Whenever my friends didn't see me in the dorm, they knew where to find me.

My first year at school ended with a special assembly. Mr. Fearon had prepared us to meet a very special guest—Helen Keller. Many of us had never met a blind person, so we were astonished that she could not see us. Still, we were thrilled to meet her. Mr. Fearon introduced each one of us. As we shook her hand, he finger-spelled our names into her palm.

I went home that summer anxious to see my family and to show off my new skills. Everyone came to our house to see a deaf girl speak. Pa asked me to recite "Our Father," but I had not practiced it, so I had a hard time. Everyone looked disappointed. Suddenly I blurted out the poem I had recited at school—"Twinkle, twinkle, little star…." The guests started talking and leaving. Pa grinned and slapped his knee.

I was glad I could speak for Pa, but just as glad I could sign, too. I enjoyed being home again, having fun like before. But I also could not wait to go back to school where I knew I had many more things to learn. Best of all, I knew that I could learn everything!